Basics of Personal Finance

How to Maintain a Financial Strategy

By

Kirk G. Meyer

Basics of Personal Finance By Kirk G. Meyer

Basics of Personal Finance

How to Maintain a Financial Strategy

Copyright © 2016 by Kirk G. Meyer

All rights reserved. This includes the right to reproduce any portion of this book in any form.

Disclaimer: Every effort was made to describe the information in this book in an accurate manner as of the publication date. The author makes no guarantees regarding the information in this book.

Why You Should Buy This Book

Anyone who is looking for some help in the area of personal finance needs to buy this book. While it may not be the longest book available it is a sleek version of longer books that cuts through the extra fluff and gives you the bare facts that you need to know to get on top of your finances. From budgeting, to banking, to paying off your debts, saving properly, how to invest with proper asset allocation and insurance. It is a one-stop book that will put you on the path to financial freedom.

Why I Wrote This Book

I wrote this book to pass along some of the information I have gathered from schooling, my life experiences and other books I have read over the years. While I could have written a much longer book I decided to go with short and sweet to get the important information across to you. There are a lot of books, and it seems that many go on and on with needless words and explanations, so I wrote this concise book to give anyone who reads it a good and solid foundation to start you on and set you on a path to financial freedom.

Basics of Personal Finance By Kirk G. Meyer

Table of Contents

Why You Should Buy This Book 3

Why I Wrote This Book 4

Table of Contents 5

Introduction 6

Budgeting 11

Banking 17

Debt Reduction 23

Emergency Funds 28

Savings 30

Retirement and Investing 33

Asset Allocation 41

Insurance 44

Conclusion 47

Thank You for Your Purchase 48

About Kirk G. Meyer 49

How to Contact Kirk G. Meyer 50

   One Last Chance for the Free Gifts! 50

Other Books by Kirk G. Meyer 51

Basics of Personal Finance By Kirk G. Meyer

Introduction

Personal finance may seem like a generic term, but it may mean many different things to different people. Some people think of personal finance and automatically think they are not equipped to handle the myriad of topics that could potentially fall under the term. Others think that no matter what it is something that they will never grasp no matter how hard they try. Others still will read countless books on the subject and may come to the conclusion that they need a professional to assist them in managing their finances. While no one of these examples is correct, not one is technically incorrect either.

Personal finance is an extremely broad and complex subject. Hundreds of thousands of books have been written on the subject, and no is not necessarily better than another. What is important is to read them and get a feel for what personal finance means to you and you alone. No one else can define what is and is not important to you in regards to your personal finance. Everyone has different financial dreams, goals, and understandings. The key is to find what it is you need in regards to personal finance and go from there.

In this book I will look at some of the more common aspects of personal finance and what makes them important. You may or may not need what I consider important, but these areas are key to understanding how to manage your personal finances. It is not the shortest book nor will it be the longest but it will be extremely useful for anyone who wants to put themselves in a better position financially.

While I have several advanced degrees, I do have one that is a Master's of Science in Financial Planning. This was my last degree, and I write this book with my course work in mind and what I know from that which is and is not important in understanding how to be successful in your financial endeavors. Now I do some financial planning as a consultant, but that does not mean that I do not think that most people can, with minimal help from a professional, manage their own finances.

First, let me state that I do believe financial planners do have their place in most people's personal finance if for no other reason to assist you in staying on the correct path and stay true to your financial plan. A financial planner is an unbiased person who can detach him or herself from the situation and assist you in maintaining the proper course of your personal finance needs. But here I do suggest that you use a fee-only financial planner and not one that makes their money off you from the sale of insurance or investments to pay their high commissions. A fee-only planner will work with you on an as-needed basis or if you hire them directly will charge a small fee based on the assets they manage on your behalf, normally about 1% of the total assets under management.

So why do I suggest you hire a fee-only planner if this book teaches you how to manage your personal finances? The answer is a simple one. In addition to helping you by being an unbiased person to assist in financial matters, a good financial planner can also provide other services that are well worth their small fees. In some instances, a financial planner can help you decide what your risk tolerance is and what in turn your asset allocation should be. We will look at this more later in the book, but these are some additional reasons why a financial planner may be worth their fees. Also, a good financial planner can help you with your tax liability by suggesting different tax strategies that will maximize the money you get to keep and minimize your tax bill. Now I am not suggesting anything illegal as I firmly believe everyone should do their duty to pay their fair share of taxes, but it is indeed unwise to pay more in taxes than you need to.

So between this book and a good fee-only financial planner that you may only need once a year or so you will be in a better position than most people to attend to and manage your finances. Again, most people can manage their finances, but they tend to think that it is too difficult, or they do not have the required education to handle the financial matters that they will be faced with. While this could be the case, it is not the case for most of us. The majority of the people I know, work with and have helped can manage their finances after they get an explanation of the basics from someone who can teach them the basics. And that is what this book is designed to do, teach you the basics of what is needed to manage your personal finances.

While this book will not cover every aspect of this vast topic, it will at a minimum prepare you to undertake to manage what you have and keep it going in the right direction. Advanced degrees are not a requirement to being successful at managing your personal finances. A college degree, in general, is not really going to help you be more successful than someone who did not graduate from college. Trust me when I say college, for the most part, did not prepare me or anyone I know how to manage their finances. Even my Financial Planning degree does not get into the basics that would help the average person. That is why this book is so valuable; it is the bare bone basics of what you need to know to have some lasting success with your personal finances. And most importantly it will help you understand when you may or may not need the help of a professional. But for the most part, if you follow what is in this book you will not need much help from a professional but rather manage your finances with a good deal of success.

If after you read this book and still need more assistance there are countless books on the subject that will in some instances go well beyond what I have covered and others will take different perspectives on the same topics covered here. But as with most things in life, there are many different ways to achieve the same results so the more you know and read the better off you will be in the long run. There are also countless blogs on the Internet that cover a wide range of topics in the area of personal finance so feel free to check those out as well. They are like the many books available; some are better than others so read them and find the ones that you can relate to and get the most benefit out of.

Thank you for purchasing this book and without any more delays let us get started with our first topic and move on from there. This book will be broken down into small sections that cover a particular topic in great detail then we will move on to the next until you finally have a solid understanding to manage your financial matters. So let us get going and start with our first topic.

Budgeting

The first step to understanding your personal finance is to understand the importance of a budget. Most people think of negative things when they hear the term budget or budgeting. But that does not have to be the case, and it does serve a very important part in your total understanding of your finances. I have read countless books on budgeting and personal finance and have heard many different theories on why you should or should not do and have a budget. But I am here to tell you that you need some form of budget system if you are to get a firm handle on your money and finances.

So why is a budget so important you may ask? Well if you have no idea where your money is going how in the world can you ever hope to understand how to save or pay off debts. So the key to all financial progress is the creation and implementation of a budget system of some kind. These can be formal or informal in nature. And what you use is up to you, but I strongly suggest some form of formal budgeting system as that will help keep you accountable for your spending and hopefully saving of excess funds.

A system that is extremely popular and endorsed by personal finance guru Dave Ramsey is the envelope system. While this is indeed a popular and effective method of budgeting you first still need to know where and how you are spending your money to a degree before setting up the envelopes. Like with any initial budget you need to know how much you will be bringing in as income sources and have a decent idea where those funds will be expended. After you have done this and I suggest a spreadsheet or at least a piece of paper with these details to set up your initial envelopes.

So you are now ready to set up the envelopes and put the cash in them for that month. This is why you need to have a good idea how much you are spending and where. Without knowing how much you spend in a category, you have no idea how much cash goes into that envelope. Now that you have the estimated cash in these envelopes you are ready to spend for that month or week or whatever you time frame is. I suggest a monthly or bi-weekly method as that is how most of us are paid. If you are paid on a different schedule such as weekly, you may distribute your cash on a weekly basis then. Use what works for you and your cash flow situation and not what is merely suggested by someone who does not fully understand your situation.

If you have a rough idea of where your cash will be spent and now have an envelope set up for that expense, you are ready to start spending for that month. Say for the ease of things that you have four envelopes, one with $500 for rent and utilities, one with $250 for groceries and eating out, one with $250 for parking and automobile expenses and one for $250 for savings. I know you will most likely have much more envelopes than this, but this is simply a sample of how the system works. Now let us say you spent all the funds in the rent and groceries envelopes and met the $250 for savings. But you have not spent all the $250 in the automobile envelope and need extra in the groceries envelope. Now you do not want to take from the savings envelope unless necessary so you will take from the automobile envelope and place that savings in the groceries envelope. You are not spending more than you have allocated to the system and are simply shifting from one envelope to another when spending necessitates this activity. This is why it is so vital that you have a good estimate of what your income and expenses will be when setting up this system. Without having a firm understanding of where your money is going, it will be extremely difficult to set up the envelopes with the proper amount of cash.

Other systems can be more or less sophisticated than the envelope system and depending on your comfort level you can choose one or a combination of these methods. If you use an informal system to track your spending that is better than not having one at all. I know many people, like my sister, who use their bank balance to budget their spending. While my sister does not have excess fees on her banking due to overdrafts, she has little overall knowledge of where she is spending her money other than looking through her bank statements. This works well for her but may not be satisfactory for someone who is saving for a down payment on a house or has large amounts of debt that they are trying to pay off. But it is adequate for someone who has little in the way of expenses and debt as my sister.

Me, I like to combine two of the next methods and use both. I track all of my income and expenses in Quicken on my laptop. It works extremely well as it allows me to see where my income is derived from and where my expenses are going. The program allows you to run many reports and will also allow you to set up a budget system in the very program itself. I must admit I have used Quicken for many years, and I have barely scratched the surface of what the program is capable of. I know you can input your bills on a recurring basis so it will remind you of when a bill is coming due. It will also allow you to view your expenses as a report and compare that to your income just as a proper budget would allow you to do. If you have any debts, the program will track those as well so you will get a better idea of where you are at in the battle with any debt you may have. And if you are one with investments the program will track those as well and give you a report that details any unrealized gains or losses you may be experiencing with your investment portfolio. All of this together can give you a pretty accurate picture of your spending and overall net worth. There are different varieties of Quicken, so I suggest you research them on a site such as Quicken's homepage or Amazon to see what one best fits your needs.

If you do not want to use the envelope system or a program such as Quicken, there are still some alternatives for you to use to meet your budgeting needs. One of them is a spreadsheet in something such as Excel. They are fairly easy to set up and use for a basic budget that allows you to track income and expenses. But they can also be fairly complex in nature as well. There are many Excel-based spreadsheets that are available for minimal costs that can track your income and expenses and then generate custom charts and reports. One of my favorite spreadsheets and the one I use is called Cash Control. It is a miniature suite of Excel spreadsheets that can be purchased for about $50 and the last I checked it had about six plus customized spreadsheets that ranged from budgets to 401(k)'s to taxes. It is an amazing group of spreadsheets and well worth the outlay of money.

The spreadsheet that you get with Cash Control will allow you to set up a budget by expense category. Just like the envelope system you need to have a basic understanding where it is your money comes from and goes but that is easily done with some planning and forethought. Then you can see how much money goes towards each expense category on a monthly basis. And this nice thing about this particular spreadsheet is you can tell it how often the expense occurs. Then it will calculate a monthly total for that particular expense. After that is set up you simply enter your expenses in the daily expense journal and it will flow back to the main spreadsheet tab. As you spend, you can check the budget against your projections and make any necessary adjustments just like you would with the envelope system. The other nice thing about this method is you can see all your totals in one easy to read view instead of going through all your envelopes or expenses if you use something like Quicken.

The last option we will examine is one that is owned by the company that owns Quicken, and that is www.mint.com. As of the publication of this book the tools of www.mint.com are free, but that can change as you know at any point in the future. I have used this as well and to be honest, I find it fascinating. On this site, you input your banking information, your retirement information, and credit card information if they are available in an on-line forum. Then Mint links to the accounts and gives you are a real-time snapshot of your finances from your bank account balance to your retirement and brokerage account balances and finally what it is you owe on your credit cards. The site will even email you when you have low balances or if a bill is coming due that has been linked to the site. While it seems the site is secure due to the fact Intuit owns and operates it, I was leery of providing all my log in information and account numbers to a third party. Though that may be more due to the fact I work for the US Government and had my personal information hacked for the third time in 17 years.

While I am not endorsing one option over the other, I do think the easiest and best for me personally is the spreadsheet method. It is easy to set up and maintain while keeping some fairly detailed information. They are easy to read and adjust as you need, and Cash Control provides a wide range of products that are all extremely useful tools in your finance quest.

Okay, now that you know where your money is from and where it is going we can move on to the next topic in your quest to get a better understanding of personal finance. And the next step is the natural one to what should come after you have your budget set up, and that is where to keep your money and how to manage it better. That is until it comes time to take your money a step further which we will look at in the following section.

Banking

Now that you know where your money will be going due to the budget you completed, it is time to look at where you keep your money. Unless you use a cash envelope system, you will need to keep your money in a bank of some sort. There are many options that are available to you now that may not have been there 10 or 15 years ago. Banking ranges from small community banks to large national banks with branches all over the country. And now credit unions have been made easier to join offering a different path to traditional banking. And now there are many on-line banks that are available to most anyone as well. So what is best for you? That depends on what it is you need from your bank and what each offers.

Traditional banks are extremely popular with most people, both large and small. The reason is there is an actual building and a network of branches that can serve your needs. This is the main reason why many people will go to a traditional bank over some of our other options. But these banks are in banking for one simple reason, to make a profit of the people it serves. Banks are not in the business of doing what may or may not be in the best interest of you, its customer. If it were, there are many services that it offers for small fees that it could offer free of charge. What you say. How do you know that you are asking? It is simple to look at the fee schedule for your traditional bank and see what is there. Yes, most banks will charge a fee to cover overdrafts as that is fairly standard practice. But not all banks charge ATM fees while others do. This could be an extremely large expense for someone who uses the ATM a lot. Bill payment systems are sometimes offered free if you have automatic deposits of your salary set up or maintain a minimum balance. The last two items are some of the ones that banks use to generate some of the billions they make in profits on an annual basis.

Also, banks will pay you a smaller interest rate on the funds you deposit with them as a rule. And then they will charge a higher interest rate when you borrow funds from them. Why is that you ask? Simply the difference between what they pay for the use of your money and what they get paid for loaning that same money out is part of their profits. Besides overdrafts fees that are generated by customers, this is most likely a bank's second largest source of income, the difference in interest paid and charged.

As for another reason bank's charge more for things that others may offer for free and the differences in interest rates traditional banks have more in the way of overhead as well in some regards. Think of it this way if you will. Bank of America has branches all over the country and in many instances many in the same community. This is not free or does this come by them cheaply. They have to pay for the site, its upkeep, the staff associated with running the branch and any other expenses associated with the operations of such a branch. As you can imagine this is not a cheap endeavor by any stretch of the imagination. It costs money and depending on the branches location and size it could cost a lot of money.

Another local option besides the traditional bank is a credit union. Credit unions are financial institutions that operate similarly to banks but with one major difference, the only allow certain groups of people to join who are then referred to as members. A second and possibly even bigger difference is that credit unions are not for profit financial institutions which mean several things for their members. Credit unions, as a rule, offer higher interest rates on the deposits that their members have with them and conversely offer lower interest rates on the money they lend out. Since they do not have to answer to shareholders or anything they are in business to serve their membership's needs. And that is done by simply offering better interest rates on deposits and lower interest rates on the loans that they make.

And unlike national banks credit unions are limited to a geographical area such as a community, county or organization. In the case of my credit union, its membership is open to the people who work for my federal agency and their immediate families. In this case, that is the criteria for membership in the credit union. But wait you say, I do not live near the credit union's service area, so this does me little good. Not true as the credit unions have established a "Shared Credit Union" network which allows me to go to any member credit union and do the same banking that I would if I were in Washington D.C. where my credit union is located. And they have these shared credit unions all over the country available to anyone's whose credit union is a member.

Another feature of many credit unions that I have experience with will offer things for free that other larger financial institutions may charge for. I am a member of two credit unions and yes they are easy to bank with and are both members of the shared network. With one I have to pay for the bill pay service if I do not maintain a certain balance or have my payroll check directly deposited with them, and the charge is minimal, $5 a month. The other credit union I bank with I do have my check deposited directly with them and I have free bill pay. Another bonus of credit union in the shared network is free ATM transactions at member locations, just like what you would expect at a national bank with numerous locations. Also, and finally, the only thing that both credit unions cost me is the cost of getting printed checks. All other things I need and use are free provided I follow the rules established by each credit union on their own.

Why can credit unions offer higher interest rates on deposits, lower rates on loans made and free services so readily? The answer I alluded to earlier is the thing that makes credit unions unique. They answer to their membership and not owners or shareholders. This means they are not out to make a profit but rather provide their membership with the best possible services through the best possible means. The result is an alternative to traditional banks and with these extra benefits. If you can look into a local credit union to see if you qualify for membership. In recent years, the laws concerning membership in credit unions have changed and in many instances, all you need is to live in the community in which the credit union is located.

A third alternative to traditional banks and credit unions are on-line banking institutions. Here you can link a traditional account at a bank or credit union to the on-line bank. Why do this you may ask? Well, they have zero or no fees associated with them, no balance restrictions, and free services or at least ones offered at a reduced rate. On-line banks will normally offer higher interest rates on deposits than even credit unions and lower interest rates on loans that they make. Like credit unions, they have lower expenses than even the credit unions as they have no physical locations that need to be maintained. And do not worry about the safety of on-line banks, if they are legitimate they are governed by the same rules as a bank and insured by the FDIC in the case of any bank failures.

I use Capital One 360 and have since before they bought Orange Direct several years ago. I will use them as an example as I am familiar with their services, but other on-line banks are similar in nature. I have both a checking and savings account with them, and a decent interest rate is paid on both accounts regardless of balance. They offer a debit card for ATM transactions and any purchases that you may want to make. Regardless of balance or anything else bill payment is free with their checking accounts. You can buy physical check from them for a nominal fee if you need to write an actual check for some reason. The only downside that I am aware of is how they handle deposits that are transferred from a linked account where the funds are held for several days before they are released. Funds deposited directly from an outside source are available immediately for use. The same is then true for transfers out of the account to a linked account; they take about three business days to complete. Other than that on-line banks are great to use to save money that you can use for emergencies or just to have it in a place that is harder to access thereby making it a little more difficult to spend on a whim.

Debt Reduction

First, let me start by stating not all debts are necessarily bad. Yes, some debts can be considered good if you stop and think about them and why you took that debt on in the first place. But let us not get ahead of ourselves. If you are like most Americans, you have some form of debt that you are responsible for. What you do with that debt and how you handle it will make the differences in your overall financial health. So we will first examine the good and bad types of debt and then how you are going to erase them, so you are financially free.

So what are the good forms of debt you are asking? That is fairly simple to answer, and I view two types are possible good debts. The first is your mortgage in your primary residence. The reason this is a good form of debt is it will generally appreciate in value over the period you will live in it. And as a secondary reason, there are some tax benefits that many people can take advantage of if they are allowed. So, if you noticed, I said your primary residence is a good form of debt, and that is key here.

On a side note, many people believe that real estate is a way to become wealthy, and it is if done properly. Taking on debts for residences that you intend to rent or lease is not a form of good debt in my opinion, and I will lay out a few of the reasons. If you can afford rental real estate you need to be aware of some of the pitfalls that it entails if you finance the properties. First no matter if the property is rented you will have a mortgage payment to make, and that is in addition to utilities and insurance that must always be maintained as well. Then you have the upkeep of the property itself and its maintenance that will always follow rental properties. For this reason alone, it is never a good idea to finance rental property as there is always an outlay of cash no matter if the property is producing any cash to pay these expenses. Now you can see that any mortgage besides your primary residence is considered as a bad form of debt.

The second form of debt that is considered a good debt by me is small amounts of student loans. Why do you ask? It is a proven fact that a college degree can increase your earning potential several times what it would have been without the degree. For this reason, I will say small amounts of student loan debt is acceptable for two reasons. The first I alluded to just a moment ago, and that is it increases your earnings potential and the second is student loans have low-interest rates and are thereby considered cheap money. Hence, why I consider student loans as a form of good debt.

So what is bad debt? That is easier to answer and explain. All other debts are bad debts as they are expensive and do not produce any tangible benefits for their use. As an example automobile loans while useful may not be in your best interest. Next to a mortgage an automobile loan will normally be your next largest expense. And unlike a house that appreciates automobiles decrease in value the moment you drive them off the lot where you purchased them. And while interest rates are still fairly low for automobiles it is still an expense that you do not need. Find a good reliable used car and purchase that hopefully using a large down payment or cash if possible. Using cash may not be an option if you are just starting out which is why I suggest a good reliable used automobile which will cost far less than a new one. Then drive it as long as you can while saving monthly what you would have spent on the loan after it is paid off. Then the next time you need a new automobile, you will have saved enough to purchase it outright and will not have to worry about a loan and to take on a bad debt.

Credit card debt is always a form of bad debt no matter what. It is never wise to purchase something on a credit card that you cannot pay off when the bill comes. The reason for this is credit cards have some of the highest interest rates that are used and it is easy to say to one's self that I will pay this off fast. Well, the best way to make that purchase if you are not going to pay the balance in full is to save for it before purchasing the item. That way you avoid the entire credit card trap in the first place. People tend not to think about the purchase as much when they use a credit card. And by that I mean they do not ask themselves the important questions such as "Can I afford this?" and "Do I need this item?" If you use cash, you are much more likely to stop yourself before the purchase and ask those questions and more. By using cash, we decrease our spending and in many instances reduce or eliminate impulse purchases.

So now that we know what debts and good and what ones are bad how do we eliminate the debts that are bad or the ones we want to be without? That is easy to answer but difficult to implement as a practice. First always pay your debts and pay them on time or your credit score will suffer the consequences. And if your credit score gets bad enough your debts will end up costing you not only late fees but higher interest rates. And no one wants that. That is the first step in getting out of debt, paying at least the minimum on all your obligations timely.

The second step is where the debts will actually get paid off, and we will examine the snowball method of reducing debts as I find that is the most effective and it really does get the job done. Here is what we need to do to start the process. First, gather all your debts in one place and list them on paper or a spreadsheet. How you list them is up to you, and we will look at the two most popular methods then I will let you in on a little secret. But gathering your debts should not take that long as you should have a really good idea of what they are as you already budgeted your monthly payments on each earlier.

Some people will need a fast victory in debt reduction so we will look at this approach first. And that is simply start paying the minimums on all your debts and pay a little extra if possible on the smallest one first. The key to all of this working is not to incur any new debts while you are paying off existing debts. If you keep getting further into debt this approach and any other approach is not going to work. So now you have paid off the smallest debt in full and have the money that was going towards that debt which will be available to be used on the next debt on your list thereby increasing the payment you will be sending into that creditor. Each time you pay off a debt you "snowball" that and the previous payments towards the next debt and it will increase each payment as each debt is paid off. You keep doing this until all of the bad debt or in some people's instances, all of your debts are paid in full.

The second approach using this method is to start with the debt that has the highest interest rate and pay that debt first. For some people, this approach may not give them that fast accomplishment feeling that paying the smallest debt first would have given you. But people like the idea of paying the highest interest debt first because it gives them a sense of saving money while they are paying off their debts.

But if the truth is told either method will work extremely well for you provided you are disciplined and avoid any new debts. And here is the best part for you, I have run sample debt paybacks of different types and interest rates with varying amounts owed. And the overall difference between the two methods is minimal when compared to an overall picture of things. So go with whatever method best suits you and will give you the encouragement to achieve your goal of becoming debt free. But the key is to create a plan for you to follow and stick to that plan.

Emergency Funds

Okay, we have got a budget to follow and developed our debt reduction plan. If you have finished repaying your debts, we can move on to an area that was touched on in the budgeting section, and that is your emergency fund. In the budgeting portion, we created a temporary emergency fund of at least $500 or better yet $1,000. Now it is time to expand that minimal fund to a full-fledged and fully funded emergency fund for you and your family.

So how much is enough when it comes to an emergency fund? That depend on you and your situation. If you are single and have an extremely stable job, your fund will be much smaller than someone who is married with a family to support and is paid on commissions. There is no one size fits all recipe for an emergency fund so it will be up to you to decide how much is enough. But there are some guidelines that most people should at least follow.

So after you have examined your situations and that of your family if you have one I would recommend at last three months' worth of expenses for a minimal emergency fund. So at a minimum, you should have three months of housing costs, automobile costs, insurance costs, food expenses, and utilities. Basically, you need what it will take you to survive for three months if you were not to have any income what so ever. In the emergency fund, I do not include debt repayment as that is the least of your concerns when you are experiencing a true emergency such as not being able to work due to illness, or you are laid off entirely.

Depending on your marketability or the severity of an illness three months may not be adequate which is why I would suggest at least six months of expenses.

So what is an emergency? As I just alluded to the loss of a job or an extended illness which makes you unable to make a living is considered an emergency. Getting new tires for an automobile is not an example of an emergency at all. That is routine maintenance. Needing a new transmission could be considered an emergency, but we will examine how that should be handled in the saving section of this book.

What is important is for you to determine what needs to be in your emergency fund and how many months you will need to save to have a fully funded fund. But a word to the wise is you can never have too much saved in your emergency fund as you never know when one will hit or how severe it may be for you and your family. And since you will have paid off your debts it should take very little time to build an adequate emergency fund.

Savings

Okay now that you have saved up an adequate emergency fund it is time to save for other things you need or desire. Money should come easier to you now that you have budgeted your earnings, paid off your debts, saved for your emergency fund and now it is time to save for other large ticket items. And of course, your investing is part of your new savings plan. But we will get to that soon. Right now we will concentrate on saving your new found excess funds.

If you own your automobile, it is now a wise idea to save what you had been paying for it on a monthly basis. And if you do take care automobile it is not unheard of for it to last you ten or more years. If you put those payments in an account for five plus years, you would be able to pay cash pretty much for your next automobile instead of financing one. Also, since you are saving this money for a new automobile if something were to happen to your current one you could use those funds to provide maintenance or pay for any repairs it may need as well. So it would be wise to have a savings account that is allocated solely for your automobile expenses and nothing else.

It would be wise also to have a savings account for your house if you do indeed own, are purchasing your house or are wanting to buy one in the future. Houses are not cheap, and the do require maintenance no matter how well you currently maintain them. Carpets need replacing every so often; rooms need to be painted as well and no matter what your roof will need to be replaced every fifteen years or so. As you can see it will easily cost you thousands of dollars over the life of your house just to maintain it in a livable condition that will also ensure that it does not lose value over time but rather will hopefully appreciate. And if you are going to purchase a house it is always a wise idea to save as much as you can for a down payment to avoid unnecessary costs as well. While it is possible to purchase a home with very little paid from your pocket towards the purchase price it is beneficial to pay at least 20% down to avoid private mortgage insurance or PMI. Several years ago PMI was paid for at least five years on a mortgage and when you reached a loan to a value where you had at least 20% of the equity in your home. Then the PMI would be removed. So if you saved the 20% down payment, you can avoid at least five years of PMI payments on your mortgage which could save you several thousands of dollars that could be applied to other things that need your attention.

That vacation to an island paradise that you want to go on? There is no need charge the trip to your credit card but rather save for it in a savings account for trips. Then once you have saved for the trip, you are free to go anywhere in the world you desire to visit and pay cash for it, and you will not incur any interest charges that everyone else will experience as they finance their trips.

As you can tell it is possible and advisable to save for any large purchase by using different savings accounts. And of course, you need to be saving for your retirement as well. Preferably you have been able to do this to a degree throughout your budgeting, debt reduction, the creation of your emergency fund, and now you will be able to turn it up a notch as well. Saving for your retirement is key to your golden years and being able to enjoy your years that do not require your going to work from 9 to 5. Next, we will examine investing and retirement accounts.

Retirement and Investing

By now you are debt free, have established a fully funded emergency fund and have been saving for any number of large ticket items. Now it is time to look at investments including retirement accounts. I hope that for this entire process you have been contributing to your employer's 401(k) plan especially is they offer a match on your contributions. But more on that later. Now that you are in a position to save and invest it is time to look at the different kinds of investment vehicles that are available to you. The three main vehicles we will examine are a typical brokerage account, an Individual Retirement Account or IRA and the workplace 401(k) or equivalent.

First, we will look at your workplace 401(k) plan if your employer offers one. If they do and they offer a company match on your contributions, I suggest the following no matter what. If you can afford it, contribute at least the amount that will receive the match from your company. Otherwise, you are giving away money, and that is never a good idea. In my case, the agency I work for will match the first 5% you contribute will match an additional 4%. That is an instant return on your money so if at all possible contribute to the match level and then worry about the debt portion of your finances. But if you are in such a position that you need every dollar available to pay the debts then that is what you must do. Then after you get a handle on the debts start contributing to your 401(k) if there is a match.

There are two types of 401(k) plans that are offered by companies. The first is the most popular and it is called a

Traditional 401(k). And this plan takes your contributions, and the company matches if there is one on a pre-tax basis. This will reduce your tax liability in the year you made the contribution, and all of the withdrawals will be taxed as ordinary income when you retire after age 55 or reach age 59 ½. At those points, you are free to make withdrawals from the 401(k) account without an early withdrawal penalty and will just owe ordinary income tax on the amounts taken out of the account. If for some reason you take an early withdrawal from the account, you will not only be taxed on the funds but will be assessed a 10% early withdrawal penalty. These accounts are set up and designed to be long-term saving instruments.

The second type of 401(k) account that is gaining in popularity with companies is the ROTH 401(k). These accounts are special in that the funds used by the contributor to fund the account are done on funds that have already been taxed. This does not reduce your tax liability in the year you make the contributions like a Traditional 401(k), but it does have some advantages. All of the funds withdrawn at retirement age are tax-free, both contributions and any earnings that the account has experienced. However, that is only the case for the employee contributions and if there is a company match those funds will be placed in a Traditional 401(k) as they have not had any taxes paid on them. They will be treated as ordinary income when they are withdrawn. However, for tax planning purposes it is a good idea to have some of each when it comes time to retire.

IRA accounts are set up similarly to 401(k) accounts in that there are several to choose from. The most common are a Traditional IRA and a ROTH IRA. They work the same as their 401(k) counterparts when it comes to tax treatment and how the withdrawals are handled. The difference here is that you are in charge of your investment choices and are not limited by the plan as you are in a 401(k). Also, the contribution limits are extremely different between these two retirement vehicles. In IRA accounts, you are allowed to contribute $5,500 if you are younger than 50 and $6,500 if you are over the age of 50. That is not a whole lot considering what you will need in retirement, but it will add up over a long period of time if you start the account early in your career. 401(k) accounts, on the other hand, allow you to contribute up to $18,000 for those under age 50 and an additional $6,000 for those over the age of 50 for a total of $24,000. As you can see 401(k) plans allow you to save much more for your retirement than an IRA account.

While 401(k) and IRA accounts are retirement accounts, there are many similarities and a few differences that need to be addressed. With a Traditional IRA, you must start to make withdrawals at age 70 and ½ no matter what. These withdrawals are sometimes referred to as Minimum Required Distributions and are the amount in the IRA divided by your life expectancy as determined by the IRS. ROTH IRA's, on the other hand, have no age restrictions for withdrawals as the taxes have already been paid in the funds that were contributed. That is the reason why Traditional IRA's have the age restriction, so the government will be able to collect its taxes that are due it from your retirement account.

With 401(k) plans, the set-up is extremely similar to that of the IRA. At age 70 and ½ you must start taking your Minimum Required Distributions from both ROTH and Traditional 401(k) plans. The exception is if you are still working at the company that holds that 401(k) you may delay withdrawals until you retire after age 70 and ½.

There are some exceptions for these retirement accounts in the event you need the funds before retirement at age 55 or age 59 and ½. With ROTH IRA's you are always able to take the principal that you contributed out at any time and provided you have had the IRA for at least five years when you reach the age of withdrawals there are no taxes owed on the funds. And there are some circumstances that allow you to withdrawal funds from any IRA such as emergency health situations, possible qualified education expenses and if you are a first time home buyer. But ideally, you will leave these funds alone and use your substantial savings ability to pay for these costs instead of reaching into your retirement accounts.

The third type of IRA account that is popular with people who are self-employed are the Simplified Employee Pension IRA or SEP IRA. These IRA's are designed for people who are truly self-employed or have self-employment income to contribute to the SEP IRA that they establish. As far as contributions the SEP IRA is more flexible than the other two IRA types in that, in theory, you have no 401(k) at work to contribute funds to. A person may contribute up to 25% of their self-employment income or $53,000 in 2015. This amount is adjusted for inflation on a regular basis so check with the Internal Revenue Service to get the latest information at www.irs.gov.

Now the third way to invest is the brokerage account. These are the last place you will want to invest after you have maxed out your IRA and 401(k) accounts. The exception is possibly the 401(k) if the plan does not offer good investment choices or is expensive to maintain due to management fees. After you decide your investment plan, the brokerage account is when you look to after the retirement accounts are maxed out.

A brokerage account is simply a way for you to buy and sell equities outside of a retirement account. These accounts are taxed on a yearly basis and do not enjoy the tax-deferred status of IRA's and 401(k) accounts. Depending on the asset you wish to buy and place in the account, it may be advantageous for the asset to be placed in a brokerage account as compared to a retirement account. If for example you find an equity that pays a dividend it may make more sense to place that security in a brokerage account where it will be taxed as a dividend and not as ordinary income. If you are in a higher tax bracket, this could mean substantial savings for you as the tax payer. Also, if you own a security for longer than a year, you will pay taxes based on the long-term capital gains tax rate and not ordinary income rates. Again, giving you the possibility to save some substantial money when it comes tax time.

There are many different ways to open and manage a brokerage account and we will examine some of them here. Some people prefer the services of a full-service brokerage house. These firms will advise you on what to buy and sell to a degree, provide research for you to help make decisions and charge higher commissions to buy and sell. Another type of brokerage firm is an on-line hybrid firm that does provide some of the services of a full-service brokerage firm if you need them but also allows you to place and utilize their on-line platform to reduce commissions and buy and sell on your own. And finally, there are strictly on-line brokerage firms that are considered discount brokers that offer minimal or no research material and no off-line assistance in your transactions. These sites are the least expensive to use and provided you do your own research and homework on your security you will be fine and using them will save you money over the long haul as they are much less expensive.

A new way to save in a brokerage account and some IRA's in robo-advisors that are becoming more and more popular with younger investors. Sites such as www.wealthfront.com, which as you a series of simple investing questions will then take your answers and develop an investing strategy for you. They then purchase exchange-traded funds to invest in and rebalance as necessary to maintain the proper asset allocation. Which is something we will examine in more detail later. While I am not endorsing Wealthfront, it is one of the older and larger robo-advisors that are available with over a billion in assets under management.

And the costs associated with these financial companies are really reasonable and are not considered excessive in nature.

Another way younger people are saving for their futures using brokerage accounts and mobile apps are companies such as Acorns. This app is unique and easy to use, and I love it as it allows me to save in small amounts with minimal effort and in such a manner I do not realize I am even investing. What this app does is you link bank accounts or credit cards to the app, and when you spend money the app will automatically perform a roundup and go to the next whole dollar amount and withdrawal that amount from your checking account to invest. Like the robo-advisor sites, you answer a series of questions to decide your asset allocation and then the app will invest each time you reach $5 or another amount that you determine. The fees associated with the use of the app are a little pricey until you reach $5,000 that is invested, costing you $1 a month until you reach that point. But it is an easy way to save some money that is designed to make it, so you do not even know you are investing or miss the funds you have invested.

There is also another type of investment I want to touch on in this section as it is similar to a retirement account but it is for qualified educational expenses, and that is a state sponsored 529 plan. First, you need to know that not all plans are equal, some offer better investment choices than others while some have lower management fees. It is best to research as many as you can to find the right plan to fit your investment style. And no you do not need to live in the state where the plan is sponsored in order to participate in that plan. Though some states will offer tax breaks and incentives if you contribute to your own state's plan, so that needs to be considered as well.

529 plans can be established for anyone that may need assistance with qualified educational expenses. Most people tend to set these up for their children or grandchildren when they are younger for college. The only problem is that unlike retirement which almost all of us will experience not everyone goes to college has a financial need if they are lucky enough to get scholarships. But the nice thing about the 529 plans are the beneficiaries of the plans may be changed so if one person does not need the funding you may designate someone else to benefit from the accumulated savings in the plan. You can even use the funds in the plan yourself provided they are for a qualified educational expense. And like a retirement account the contributions grow tax-deferred until they are withdrawn. And provided that they are withdrawn for qualified educational expenses, the funds are tax-free, both the contributions and any earnings that they made.

So what do you do if you start a 529 plan and end up having no beneficiary at all to name for the plan? Well, it then becomes similar to an IRA account or a 401(k) where you take the money out before your retirement or age 59 and ½. There is a 10% penalty that you must pay in addition to ordinary taxes on any gains that may have been realized at the time you liquidated the account.

Asset Allocation

Okay, now you have set up your investments and have a plan on what it is you wish to have in your portfolio. The question is what is it you need in your portfolio to achieve your goals? The answer to that question is the proper asset allocation across all of your investments, retirement, brokerage and even a state-sponsored 529 plan for education if you have one established. When it comes to asset allocation, you need to consider all of your assets that are invested. I would not consider your primary residence as real estate for this purpose as it is not an asset that produces an income or one that you are likely to use as a realized gain as it is where you live, not some rental property.

So what are the assets that people invest in you may ask? Well, the list is limitless and for some, it can be as creative as they can be. For others, it is as simple as cash, equities, and bonds. But it is possible to invest in just about anything nowadays with the use of mutual funds and exchange-traded funds. These financial assets can be a collection of real estate that pools all of the tenants rents together and pays out in the form of a Real Estate Investment Trust or REIT. There are exchange-traded funds that invest in precious metals such as silver and gold. Numerous funds invest in a variety of bonds that are issued by domestic or foreign governments all the way to high-risk corporate bonds that have a high degree of risk associated with them. People can even place rental properties in IRA's that have a custodian to manage them. All of these are different types of assets that people can consider when developing investment plans and asset allocation plans for their portfolios.

In previous years, most people who prepared for retirement tended to use only three asset classes for their needs. And then people tended to be a bit conservative with those assumptions. As people live longer, they need to rethink their asset allocation. It was widely thought you should own your age in bonds and the difference to a hundred in equities. That means if you were 60 years old you should have a portfolio that was 60% bonds and 40% equities. The only problem with this take is you may outlive your funds as people need more in equities to continue to increase their portfolio ahead of inflation. In today's world and with people living longer it does not make sense to have large quantities of cash and bonds in one's portfolio. People need the growth power of equities or other assets to make up the difference in their portfolio's value.

There are some on-line tools that you can Google to see what asset allocation best fits your risk tolerance level. The more risk you can tolerate the more aggressive your asset allocation will be. Also, the younger you are, the more aggressive you can stand to be as well as you will have time on your side to make any recoveries that may need to be made due to an asset's poor performance. But studies have shown that the more diversified one is, the better off they will be if one or two assets turn out to be down at any point in time. Also, by diversifying your assets you can increase your overall return while significantly reducing your portfolio's risk. Think about that for a few moments; you can reduce risk and increase your returns with a well thought out asset allocation plan. If you do not feel comfortable doing this yourself, I can completely understand. With so many asset classes to choose from and trying to figure out your risk tolerance, it can be daunting indeed. Also, many people find it difficult to pick assets as they may have preconceived ideas about one asset over another. This is where a fee-only financial advisor can come in extremely handy. They can help you pick the assets that best fit your risk tolerance and investment strategy for you. They can also explain why or how an asset class can benefit your needs when it may not be readily apparent to you. Then all you have to do is visit them on an annual basis to keep things on track and readjust your asset allocation balances. In reality, this is some money that can be well spent and some that I do not consider to be wasted in the least.

Insurance

A lot of people do not think of insurance as part of their financial lives and in fact many books do not even include a section on the subject. But I am here to tell you that there are many different types of insurance that you need to consider when thinking about your financial health. Unless you can do what people refer to as self-insure you have a need for insurance, and most likely many different types of insurance.

So why do you need insurance? It is simply a form of risk management. For those things that you do not want to take the risk on you purchase insurance to do that for you. As I alluded to a moment ago, people purchase insurance to reduce the monetary risk that they are willing to take on any number of things. We will look at some of the more common forms of insurance that most people have in place.

With the passage of the Affordable Health Care Act, everyone is now required to have health insurance. This is a fairly common insurance for people and one that is vital in my opinion. Until about two or three years ago I was fairly lucky and had not had many medical issues but in the span of about 16 months, I had three surgeries and corresponding hospital stays. The one that sticks out in my mind was the first that was about ten days in length. Not that long but not short either. Well, that one stay cost me about $500 out of pocket with my insurance, well within an amount I could afford. But the hospital billed my insurance company over $100,000 for that ten-day stay, and they paid about $35,000 to the hospital and doctors. That is over $100,000 I would have been responsible for had I not had health insurance. So the premiums and the co-pays over my 17 years with the government were justified with that single surgery and hospital stay. Now you can see it is about managing risks that you cannot or do not want to pay for yourself.

Automobile insurance is another that is mandatory in most states, or at least the liability portion is. But if you did not pay cash for your automobile you will be required by the financial institution that loaned you the money to carry not only liability insurance but collision and comprehensive coverage as well. That is so that the finance company is guaranteed it will recover its investment in the event there is some accident. And with the way people sue these days it is wise to have insurance in the event you cause an accident and hurt someone. If that is the case, the liability portion of your policy will cover you, in many instances up to several hundred thousand of dollars' worth of coverage.

Life insurance is another insurance where you are managing a degree of risk. If you are young and have a family, there is a risk that you may die and leave your family in a position that is not desirable financially. That is why people buy life insurance, to protect their loved ones that may depend on them for some financial need. For younger people I would suggest getting a term policy for 20 or 30 years when you start your family for an amount that will allow them to be comfortable after your passing until they can get on their own feet without you. And the great thing about term life insurance is if you buy a house and do not want your family to worry about the mortgage payments you simply buy a policy to cover the cost of the house for the life of the mortgage. Have kids that will go to college? Buy a term policy when they are born for 20 years to cover the cost of their education in the event you pass away at a young age. The nice thing about term policies is that they are fairly inexpensive and are flexible to use. In fact, you can manage risks on a number of things with a few term life insurance policies.

Homeowner's insurance is another insurance similar to automobile insurance when your house is financed, as it will be required by your financial institution that lent you the funds to purchase the house to protect them against any loss. And most people will have insurance on their contents in conjunction with their homeowner's policy to insure the contents of their house. And for people that rent there is renters insurance that will cover your property inside of your residence.

The final type of insurance that we will examine is a policy that works with your homeowner's or automobile policies, and that is an umbrella liability policy. This policy will increase your liability coverage for a minimal cost. In the case of my policy, it is for a million dollars in liability coverage in addition to what my automobile and homeowner's policies will pay. And the best past is it is not an expensive policy to purchase, mine is about $150 annually for the million in additional liability coverage.

Conclusion

I have not covered all of the possible topics of personal finance in this book, but I have provided you with enough information to start down a path of financial freedom. Some people know the things covered in this book while for others it may be new information. Most of what I have written about in this book comes from my schooling, my life experiences and as I started earlier what I have read in other books. But taken as a whole the information that I have provided can and will place you in a position to set yourself up for financial freedom that without some basic understanding you would not be able to achieve. And I hope that this book provided you with the basics to get your financial life in order.

Thank You for Your Purchase

Thank you for purchasing this book, and I hope you found it useful in your journey to financial freedom. Please leave me a comment if you liked the book on Amazon at http://amzn.to/291CkcK.

If there is anything that you think I can improve on, please feel free to contact me and let me know and I will take all comments into consideration for future revisions of the book. You can find my contact information in the following section.

About Kirk G. Meyer

Kirk G. Meyer's educational and work background is fairly diverse. He holds a BS in Business Administration from Haskell Indian Nations University in Lawrence, Kansas and an MBA and MS in Accounting from Strayer University in Washington, DC. He just finished the final course in an MS in Financial Planning from Bentley University in suburban Boston, Massachusetts. Mr. Meyer works for the federal government in the area of contracts and before his current position was a bank examiner for a federal regulatory agency. In addition to his education and work experience, he is also a registered independent life insurance agent in his home state of Tennessee, selling various life insurance and annuities to individuals and families in need of these types of products. His educational background and love of helping others make him an asset to those looking for assistance and guidance in financial and personal financial matters.

How to Contact Kirk G. Meyer

Feel free to email Kirk at kirk@kirkgmeyer.com.

Please follow Kirk's blog at www.kirkgmeyer.com and he welcomes any comments or suggestions on how to make his blog or eBooks better for you.

You can also follow Kirk on Twitter at @kirkgmeyer

You can follow Kirk on Facebook at www.facebook.com/kirkgmeyer

You can follow Kirk on LinkedIn at www.linkedin.com/in/kirkgmeyer

For a complete listing of Kirk's books, please visit his Amazon Author Page at Kirk G Meyer.

One Last Chance for the Free Gifts!

Again, as a big thank you for getting Basics of Personal Finance, I want to offer you some valuable free gifts and a chance to get some on-going financial advice. Just for getting this book it entitles you to my Budget Spreadsheet and Debt Reduction Spreadsheet that I normally sell for a total of $10. It is yours free for getting Basics of Personal Finance and signing up for my free email newsletters that have previews to my ebooks, special articles that are geared towards personal finance and now access to these two valuable spreadsheets. To get your spreadsheets now simply go to my blogs website and sign up today. Visit www.kirkgmeyer.com today to get your free valuable spreadsheets.

Other Books by Kirk G. Meyer

Thrift Savings Plan: A Practical Guide to the TSP

The Basics of Life Insurance

A Brief Overview of Annuities

Financial Plans: Just the Basics

Personal Finance: A Grouping of Financial Topics

Final Expense Insurance

Budgeting 101

The Basics of Life Insurance and Annuities Bundle

Your Credit Report and You

www.ingramcontent.com/pod-product-compliance
Lightning Source LLC
Chambersburg PA
CBHW070411190526
45169CB00003B/1205